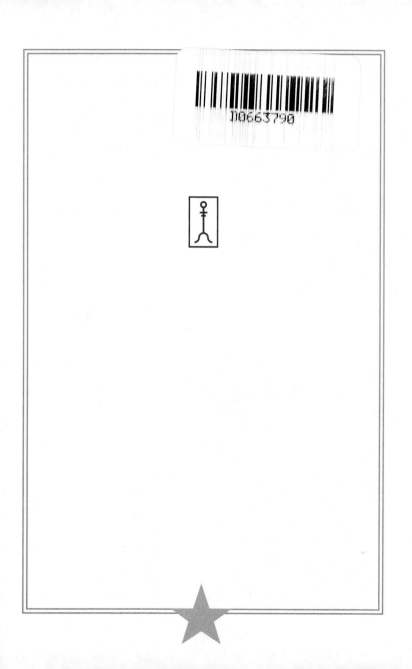

George W. Bushisms

NEW WAYS TO HARM OUR COUNTRY

Jacob Weisberg

A FIRESIDE BOOK
Published by Simon & Schuster
New York   London   Toronto   Sydney

FIRESIDE
Rockefeller Center
1230 Avenue of the Americas
New York, NY 10020

FIRESIDE and colophon are registered
trademarks of Simon & Schuster, Inc.

For information regarding special discounts
for bulk purchases, please contact
Simon & Schuster Special Sales at 1-800-456-6798
or business@simonandschuster.com.

DESIGNED BY JILL WEBER

Manufactured in the United States of America
1 3 5 7 9 10 8 6 4 2
ISBN-13: 978-0-7432-7689-4
ISBN-10: 0-7432-7689-2

Foreword

BY CALVIN TRILLIN

While George W. Bush was running for president in 2000, I wrote a poem entitled "A Scientific Observation on the Speaking Problems That Seem to Run in the Bush Family":

> He thinks that *hostile's hostage.*
> He cannot say *subliminal.*
> The way Bush treats the language
> Is bordering on criminal.
>
> His daddy had the problem:
> He used the nounless predicate.
> Those cowboy boots can do that
> To people from Connecticut.

If we subject this poem to close textual analysis—
something, I must admit, that nobody has ever both-
ered to do with any of my poems before—we can see
clearly that it makes two points. For one, the mangled
syntax that has made George W. Bush, the forty-third

president of the United States, a laughingstock in some quarters and has made Jacob Weisberg, the editor of these enormously popular books of Bushisms, a billionaire several times over, is shown to exist in at least two generations of the Bush family. Since no one questions the intelligence of George H. W. Bush—who was, after all, elected to Phi Beta Kappa—this amounts to a refutation of the theory that the younger Bush speaks the way he does because he's not smart enough to speak any other way. That theory has always had strong proponents, particularly after details of George W. Bush's academic record and his business career began to leak out, but, speaking personally, I am happy to be rid of it. I think it's dispiriting to discuss whether or not the president of the United States—what used to be called the leader of the Free World until the Patriot Act and Guantanamo Bay made that phrase sound sarcastic—is simply a doofus.

The second point is hinted at by the word "scientific" in the poem's title. Rereading that title a few years after it was written, I realized that I had postulated what scientists call a hypothesis—the hypothesis that cramming the feet of high-born Eastern-seaboard preppies into cowboy boots can lead to speech difficulties. Far-fetched, you say? It isn't so far, in fact, from the hypothesis that forcing a naturally left-handed child to become right-handed can lead to stuttering or, for that matter, from the hypothesis I concocted some years ago to see if I could cause a brief panic on Wall Street—that wearing red suspenders instead of a belt can lower the sperm count.

Once I realized that my cowboy-boots breakthrough was a hypothesis, I was surprised that there had been no significant response from the scientific community. As I have always understood the scientific method, once someone postulates a hypothesis, researchers test it through such devices as laboratory experiments, longitudinal studies, and—in this case, I would assume—extensive interviews with a significant sampling of boot salesmen in places like Lubbock and Wichita Falls ("Yes, sir, when he first came in here—walked in wearing some of them Docksiders, they call 'em, with no socks—he was talkin' away just as pretty as you please . . . .") I know that President George W. Bush himself has spoken out vigorously for thoroughness in scientific investigation—global warming and evolution are just two of the areas where he has indicated that there is considerable work left to be done before the verdict is in—and yet there has been no sustained effort to test my hypothesis.

I had assumed that, at the very least, some of those hotshot Washington reporters would use my poem as a takeoff point for the sort of probing questions they like to trot out for televised press conferences. Is it true, for instance, that those members of the Bush clan who remained in what the geopolitical types might call "the Greenwich Country Day sphere of influence" express themselves with great fluidity, except for those who keep their teeth tightly clenched in the high-WASP delivery sometimes referred to as Locust Valley lockjaw? Or is a breakdown in sentence structure a widespread Old Money affectation, like frayed button-downs and peeling paint? Could it be that one of the secret rituals of Skull and Bones is foot binding? If cowboy boots have no effect on behavior or syntax, why do western ranch hands refer to a visitor from the East as a tenderfoot? Where does the penny loafer stand in all of this?

When it comes to the answers to these questions, I am willing to let the chips fall where they may. I'm aware that some people will say that I am making too much of the effect cowboy boots could have on what I think could be fairly described as effete feet. They will argue that although a drastic change of footwear could conceivably affect pronunciation and fluidity, it could never cause the sort of thought process that brings George W. Bush to utter a sentence like "Free societies will be allies against these hateful few who have no conscience, who kill at the whim of a hat," or the sentence that inspired the subtitle of this book: "Our enemies will never stop searching for new ways to harm our country, and neither will I."

But footwear is symbolic of a much broader cultural dislocation suffered by the Bush family. These are people who switched rather suddenly from finger sandwiches to fried pork rinds, and then switched back again every summer when they returned to Kennebunkport. These are people who grew up listening to pleasant Episcopalian vicars sermonize on the need to be kind to one's servants and now find themselves locked in a partnership with preachers like Jerry Falwell, who believes that God calls up hurricanes to

smite those who demonstrate a tolerance of The Homosexual Lifestyle.

What must have been the most wrenching switch came in 1980, when, after decades of being prominent supporters of Planned Parenthood and other pro-choice efforts, the entire Bush family became militantly antiabortion in about thirty seconds—the approximate amount of time it took George H. W. Bush to decide that he would be willing to reverse his deeply held views on the issue as a condition for becoming Ronald Reagan's running mate. And, in common parlance, what would be one way to describe the abruptness of that change? That's right: so fast it left you *speechless*.

Could it be that if the Bush family had been given the luxury of making this and other cultural changes more gradually, both of the Bush presidents would be speaking in perfectly parsed paragraphs and Jacob Weisberg would still be a humble scribbler without even one 727 to his name? I offer as evidence for the affirmative William Jefferson Clinton, of Hot Springs, Arkansas. Clinton must have known what could happen to the rhetorical skills of someone who, as they say in the South, "strayed too far from his raisin'." Despite his gold-chip education, he clung to the culture of Arkansas so tightly that his Secret Service code name was Bubba and it was easy to imagine him in the Oval Office at about nine-thiry in the morning swigging a ten-ounce bottle of Coke with goobers in it. Yes, of course, the man had his faults as president. But he spoke like an angel.

day sounding like Gore Vidal. In the past, specialists have speculated that Bush suffers from some sort of genetic malady like dyslexia or apraxia. That kind of thing doesn't just clear up spontaneously, like a case of teen acne, at fifty-eight.

We must not discount the possibility of a conspiracy at the highest reaches of the government. To date, no one has explained the mysterious rectangular bulge and wire observed beneath Bush's suit coat at the first debate in Miami. Yes, this could have been some sort of medical or security device. But the box could also have transmitted a grammatical conservative voice for Bush to echo. Arguing against this theory is that the bulge hasn't reappeared. But perhaps the device has been . . . *implanted*.

A more plausible explanation is that Bush's inarticulacy has always been to some degree a pose. There's no question but that he amps up his regular guy–ness and anti-intellectualism on certain occasions. But during the election and since, Bush has had reason to amp them down. Running against a haughty, hyperarticulate Boston Brahmin pulled Bush to the linguistic center. Now that he's ineligible to run again, it's safe for

Introduction

BY JACOB WEISBERG

This year disaster struck the Bushisms project, when the President began speaking English. The phenomenon was first observed during the summer of 2004, in the midst of a presidential campaign that should have had George W. gibbering and sputtering the way he had in 2000. At the outset, the signs were subtle. Bush's "hunnert" flattened almost imperceptibly into an articulated "hundred," his "garmint" into a trisyllabic "government." During the debates, Bush sounded almost fluent. Though he flat ran out of things to say halfway into his first showdown with John Kerry, he hardly stumbled at all.

After the inauguration, the situation continued to deteriorate. Bush held a nearly flawless press conference. On a fence-mending trip to Europe, he delivered an eloquent speech citing Leibniz, Newton, and Camus, the latter's name pronounced without a final "s." I'd been noticing this trend with alarm when the *Wall Street Journal* weighed in with a front-pager on the subject. "He is enunciating more clearly and dotting his remarks with more literary references," a reporter named John McKinnon noted of Bush. My little problem was out of the bag.

Some of Bush's literary references appear to come from . . . reading. Bush informed an interviewer that he was immersed in Natan Sharansky's *The Case for Democracy* (though when he met the author, he did acknowledge that he hadn't finished it). He told friends he loved Tom Wolfe's *I Am Charlotte Simmons* (though six months later, he was still hefting it around). Aides

noted that he was working his way through biographies of George Washington and Alexander Hamilton. To Bryan Lamb of C-SPAN, Bush even sung the praises of reading in bed. "Twenty pages later you're out cold," he said.

What the Kennebunkport is going on here?

Adult-onset literacy violates what we know of psychology and even physiology. People can learn to read at any age, but Yogi Berra does not wake up on Wednes-

Bush to be himself—a bit of a yahoo, to be sure, but not the populist bumpkin he sometimes pretends to be.

There's also the muzzle factor. During the campaign, Karl Rove wasn't taking any chances. Bush was allowed to appear in public for the most part only in scripted settings. Even after the election, the president's Social Security "conversations" were stacked with carefully vetted supporters, who offered up pre-screened questions. By April, though, Bush was again appearing at more spontaneous events and his output of Bushisms increased correspondingly.

Finally, it must be admitted that Bush has simply improved with practice. If you have no ear for music, four years of piano lessons won't turn you into Duke Ellington. But it would be amazing if it didn't make you a better, even a passable pianist. Why should being president and trying to speak English be any different?

Luckily for me, a comment doesn't have to be flubbed or ungrammatical to qualify as a "Bushism." From the beginning, I've included in these anthologies statements by the president that while indisputably correct in terms of sentence structure and noun-verb agreement are nonetheless amusing or terrifying, depending on your perspective, because of what they reveal about the inner man. (To the top of the heap in this edition: "I trust God speaks through me.") In such cases, the concern is that the president may in fact have said precisely what he did mean.

In this habit of occasionally scaring us silly by speaking his true mind, Bush has some company inside his administration. In particular, his two most powerful lieutenants, Dick Cheney and Donald Rumsfeld, do it too. This edition features the best of what you might call their Bushisms-by-proxy.

As with Bush, the offhand comments of Cheney and Rummy reflect sides of their characters usually kept hidden. Rumsfeld's intermittent candor, which often strikes partway into his Pentagon press conferences, invariably creates a "meta" moment. Rummyisms highlight the fundamental absurdity of the SecDef's position, while conveying a curious, Zenlike serenity at the core of someone who is frequently misunderstood as a simple bully (he's actually a complicated bully). Cheneyisms, by contrast, broadcast the bottled-up bitterness of the most powerful man in the world. For a brief moment, the number 2 drops his placid mask (along with the mask that he's a number 2), in order to emit a ghoulish, *mwha-ha-ha* cackle.

These politically inappropriate feelings—Rummy's *Goodness gracious, what I'm saying is ridiculous* and Cheney's *I can crush you like a bug*—are aspects of Bush's persona as well. Like any good executive, the man knows how to delegate.

LOVING HUSBAND

"I appreciate my love for Laura."

—*Washington, D.C., April 20, 2005*

LOVING DOCTOR

"Too many good docs are getting out of the business. Too many OB/GYNs aren't able to practice their love with women all across the country."

—*Polar Bluff, Missouri, September 6, 2004*

1

BLACK HATS

"Free societies are hopeful societies. And free societies will be allies against these hateful few who have no conscience, who kill at the whim of a hat."

—Washington, D.C., September 17, 2004

OVERKILL

"They've got people there that are willing to kill, and they're hard-nosed killers. And we will work with the Iraqis to secure their future."

—Washington, D.C., April 28, 2005

HARMLESS

"It's in our country's interests to find those who would do harm to us and get them out of harm's way."

—Washington, D.C., April 28, 2005

HARMFUL

"Our enemies are innovative and resourceful, and so are we. They never stop thinking about new ways to harm our country and our people, and neither do we."

—Washington, D.C., August 5, 2004

DEFINITION

"We've investigated every single complaint against the detainees. It seemed like to me they based some of their decisions on the word of—and the allegations—by people who were held in detention, people who hate America, people that had been trained in some instances to disassemble—that means not tell the truth."

—Washington, D.C., May 31, 2005

CIVICS

"They can get in line like those who have been here legally and have been working to become a citizenship in a legal manner."

—Referring to immigrant workers, Washington, D.C., December 20, 2004

BLESSINGS

"And so during these holiday seasons,
we thank our blessings. . . ."

—*Fort Belvoir, Virginia, December 10, 2004*

MOO

"I believe that, as quickly as possible, young cows ought to be allowed to go across our border."

—Ottawa, Canada, November 30, 2004

A NEW PAGE

"[I'm] occasionally reading, I want you to know, in the second term."

—Washington, D.C., March 16, 2005

NOT IT

"We need to apply twenty-first-century information technology to the health care field. We need to have our medical records put on the I.T."

—Collinsville, Illinois, January 5, 2005

DRAFT I

"I hear there's rumors on the Internets
that we're going to have a draft."

—*St. Louis, Missouri, October 8, 2004*

DRAFT II

"After standing on the stage, after the debates,
I made it very plain, we will not have an
all-volunteer army. And yet, this week—we will
have an all-volunteer army. Let me restate that."

—*Daytona Beach, Florida, October 16, 2004*

THE ULTIMATE SACRIFICE

"I want to appreciate those of you who wear
our nation's uniform for your sacrifice."

—*Jacksonville, Florida, January 14, 2005*

LOST

"It's a time of sorrow and sadness
when we lose a loss of life."

—Washington, D.C., December 21, 2004

ARMS AND THE MEN

"That's why I went to the Congress last September and proposed fundamental—supplemental funding, which is money for armor and body parts and ammunition and fuel."

—Erie, Pennsylvania, September 4, 2004

EXTENDING A HAND

"I'm honored to shake the hand of a brave Iraqi citizen who had his hand cut off by Saddam Hussein."

—Washington, D.C., May 25, 2004

UNSANCTIONED

"Secondly, the tactics of our—as you know, we don't have relationships with Iran. I mean, that's—ever since the late seventies, we have no contacts with them, and we've totally sanctioned them. In other words, there's no sanctions—you can't—we're out of sanctions."

—Annandale, Virginia, August 9, 2004

SANCTIONED

"This notion that the United States is getting ready to attack Iran is simply ridiculous. And having said that, all options are on the table."

—Brussels, Belgium, February 22, 2005

GET ME WRITE

"He understands the need for a timely
write of the constitution."

—*on Prime Minister Ibrahim Jaafari of Iraq,*
Washington, D.C., April 28, 2005

GET ME REWRITE

"And there is a new history now that that has been done,
and that history needs to be included in the process."

—*Bratislava, Slovakia, February 24, 2005*

YESTERDAY

"We discussed the way forward in Iraq, discussed the
importance of a democracy in the greater Middle East
in order to leave behind a peaceful tomorrow."

—*Tbilisi, Georgia, May 10, 2005*

14

STOCK TIP

"[A] free Iraq is essential to our respective securities."

—Washington, D.C., June 1, 2004

RUN

"I like the idea of people running for office. There's a positive effect when you run for office. Maybe some will run for office and say, vote for me, I look forward to blowing up America. I don't know, I don't know if that will be their platform or not. But it's—I don't think so. I think people who generally run for office say, vote for me, I'm looking forward to fixing your potholes, or making sure you got bread on the table."

—On elections in the Middle East,
Washington, D.C., March 16, 2005

A PIECE OF THE ACTION

"Well, we've made the decision to defeat the terrorists abroad so we don't have to face them here at home. And when you engage the terrorists abroad, it causes activity and action."

—*Washington, D.C., April 28, 2005*

INTELLIGENCE

"The CIA laid out several scenarios and said life could be lousy, life could be OK, life could be better, and they were just guessing as to what the conditions might be like."

—*On Iraq after the occupation,*
New York, September 21, 2004

HOPE

"I saw a poll that said the right track/wrong track in Iraq was better than here in America. It's pretty darn strong. I mean, the people see a better future."

—Washington, D.C., September 23, 2004

JUSTICE

"I didn't join the International Criminal Court because I don't want to put our troops in the hands of prosecutors from other nations. Look, if somebody has done some wrong in our military, we'll take care of it. We got plenty of capability of dealing with justice."

—Niceville, Florida, August 10, 2004

FACTS

"Part of the facts is understanding we have a problem, and part of the facts is what you're going to do about it."

—Kirtland, Ohio, April 15, 2005

OPTIMISM

"And I am an optimistic person. I guess if you want to try to find something to be pessimistic about, you can find it, no matter how hard you look, you know?"

—Washington, D.C., June 15, 2004

OPTIMISM II

"I believe we are called to do the hard work to make our communities and quality of life a better place."

—Collinsville, Illinois, January 5, 2005

24

ANOTHER COUNTRY

"After all, Europe is America's closest ally."

—Mainz, Germany, February 23, 2005

ISOLATIONISM

"We thought we were protected forever from trade policy or terrorist attacks because oceans protected us."

—Speech to business leaders at APEC Summit, Santiago, Chile, November 20, 2004

DARK FUTURE

"Coal also prevents an environmental challenge"

—Washington, D.C., April 20, 2005

JUST SAY NO

"The president and I also reaffirmed our determination to fight terror, to bring drug trafficking to bear, to bring justice to those who pollute our youth."

—Speaking with Chilean president Ricardo Lagos,
Santiago, Chile, November 21, 2004

I MEANT WHAT
I MEANT

"Tribal sovereignty means that, it's sovereign. You're a—you've been given sovereignty, and you're viewed as a sovereign entity. And, therefore, the relationship between the federal government and tribes is one between sovereign entities."

—Washington, D.C., August 6, 2004

I MEANT WHAT THAT MEANT

"In terms of timetables, as quickly as possible—whatever that means."

—On the president's time frame for shoring up Social Security, Washington, D.C., March 16, 2005

PROMISES, PROMISES

"I think younger workers—first of all, younger workers have been promised benefits the government— promises that have been promised, benefits that we can't keep. That's just the way it is."

—Washington, D.C., May 4, 2005

28

INCALCULABLE I

"Because the—all which is on the table begins to address the big cost drivers. For example, how benefits are calculated, for example, is on the table; whether or not benefits rise based upon wage increases or price increases. There's a series of parts of the formula that are being considered.

And when you couple that, those different cost drivers, affecting those—changing those with personal accounts, the idea is to get what has been promised more likely to be—or closer delivered to what has been promised. Does that make any sense to you? It's kind of muddled."

—Explaining his plan to save Social Security,
Tampa, Florida, February 4, 2005

INCALCULABLE II

"Look, there's a series of things that cause the—like, for example, benefits are calculated based upon the increase of wages, as opposed to the increase of prices. Some have suggested that we calculate—the benefits will rise based upon inflation, as opposed to wage increases. There is a reform that would help solve the red if that were put into effect. In other words, how fast benefits grow, how fast the promised benefits grow, if those—if that growth is affected, it will help on the red."

—Explaining his plan to save Social Security,
Tampa, Florida, February 4, 2005

GROWTH

"It means your own money would grow better than that which the government can make it grow. And that's important."

—On what private accounts could do for Social Security, Falls Church, Virginia, April 29, 2005

FIX THIS

"I repeat, personal accounts do not permanently fix the solution."

—Washington, D.C., March 16, 2005

33

WORKING

"We got people working all their life at hard work, contributing by payroll taxes into a Social Security system."

—Washington, D.C., May 13, 2005

EXPIRATION

"If they pre-decease or die early, there's an asset base to be able to pass on to a loved one."

—On Social Security money stored in private accounts, Cedar Rapids, Iowa, March 30, 2005

MR. MOM

"I'm going to spend a lot of time on Social Security. I enjoy it. I enjoy taking on the issue. I guess it's the mother in me."

—Washington, D.C., April 14, 2005

35

TRANSGENDERED

"I want to thank my friend, Senator Bill Frist, for joining us today. . . . He married a Texas girl, I want you to know. Karyn is with us. A West Texas girl, just like me."

—Nashville, Tennessee, May 27, 2004

TRANSGENDERED II

"If you're a younger person, you ought to be asking members of Congress and the United States Senate and the president what you intend to do about it. If you see a train wreck coming, you ought to be saying, what are you going to do about it, Mr. Congressman, or Madam Congressman?"

—Detroit, Michigan, February 8, 2005

HUGS

"They've seen me make decisions, they've seen me under trying times, they've seen me weep, they've seen me laugh, they've seen me hug. And they know who I am, and I believe they're comfortable with the fact that they know I'm not going to shift principles or shift positions based upon polls and focus groups."

—Interview with **USA Today,** *August 27, 2004*

KISSES

"I always jest to people, the Oval Office is the kind of place where people stand outside, they're getting ready to come in and tell me what for, and they walk in and get overwhelmed by the atmosphere. And they say 'Man, you're looking pretty.' "

—Washington, D.C., November 4, 2004

40

MIRROR, MIRROR, ON THE WALL

"In this job you've got a lot on your plate on a regular basis; you don't have much time to sit around and wander, lonely, in the Oval Office, kind of asking different portraits, 'How do you think my standing will be?' "

—Washington, D.C., March 16, 2005

ON THE MEDIA

"We look forward to analyzing and working with legislation that will make—it would hope—put a free press's mind at ease that you're not being denied information you shouldn't see."

—Washington, D.C., April 14, 2005

ON THE MEDIA II

"Listen, whoever thought about modernizing this room deserves a lot of credit. Like, there's very little oxygen in here anymore."

—On the confines of the White House's Brady Press Briefing Room, Washington, D.C., March 16, 2005

THAT LITTLE VOICE

"I understand there's a suspicion that we—we're too security-conscience."

—Washington, D.C., April 14, 2005

TEACHINGS

"I want to thank you for the importance that you've shown for education and literacy."

—*Washington, D.C., April 13, 2005*

TEACHINGS II

"We expect the states to show us whether or not we're achieving simple objectives—like literacy, literacy in math, the ability to read and write."

—*On federal education requirements, Washington, D.C., April 28, 2005*

TEACHINGS III

"We must continue the work of education reform to bring high standards and accountability, not just to our elementary and secondary schools, but to our high schools as well."

—*Washington, D.C., November 4, 2004*

FUNDING

"I mean, if you've ever been a governor of a state, you understand the vast potential of broadband technology, you understand how hard it is to make sure that physics, for example, is taught in every classroom in the state. It's difficult to do. It's, like, cost-prohibitive."

—Washington, D.C., June 24, 2004

EVOLUTION

"So community colleges are accessible, they're available, they're affordable, and their curriculums don't get stuck. In other words, if there's a need for a certain kind of worker, I presume your curriculums evolved over time."

—Niceville, Florida, August 10, 2004

SYSTEMIC PROBLEM

"And that's why I'm here at the community college system today."

—Jacksonville, Florida, January 14, 2005

47

VOICE OF GOD

"I trust God speaks through me.
Without that, I couldn't do my job."

—*To a group of Amish, as quoted by the*
Lancaster New Era, *July 9,* **2004**

VOICE OF GOD II

"I'm also mindful that man should never try to
put words in God's mouth. I mean, we should
never ascribe natural disasters or anything
else, to God. We are in no way, shape, or
form should a human being play God."

—*Appearing on ABC's* 20/20,
Washington, D.C., January 14, **2005**

SAY IT AGAIN

"See, in my line of work you got to keep repeating things over and over and over again for the truth to sink in, to kind of catapult the propaganda."

—*Greece, New York, May 24, 2005*

MONOLOGUE

"I can only speak to myself."

—*Washington, D.C., April 28, 2005*

50

Cheneyisms

OIL

"Let us rid ourselves of the fiction that low oil prices are
somehow good for the United States."

—Washington, D.C., October 1986

ELECTRICITY

"If you want to leave all the lights on in your house, you can. There's no law against it. But you will pay for it."

—Washington, D.C., May 19, 2001

GAS

"Conservation may be a sign of personal virtue, but it is not a sufficient basis for a sound, comprehensive energy policy."

—Toronto, Canada, April 30, 2001

NUCLEAR

"Denuclearization is not a good idea."

—United Press International, May 8, 1990

54

DON'T GET YOUR HOPES UP

"You don't want to take the oath of office
and find out the report was wrong."

*—On why his first move, if told the president had died,
would be to verify that he was actually dead.*
Time, *October 17, 2000*

HEALTHY

"Except for the occasional heart attack,
I never felt better."

—Washington, D.C., June 4, 2003

PRIORITIES

"I had other priorities in the sixties
than military service."

—The Washington Post, *April 5, 1989*

THE WHITE HOUSE PROPOSES

"Fuck yourself."

—*To Senator Patrick J. Leahy during a Senate photo session,
as quoted by* The Washington Post,
Washington, D.C., June 25, 2004

BIG TIME

"Oh, yeah. He is. Big time."

—*Responding to Govenor George W. Bush after Bush called a*
New York Times *reporter a "major league asshole,"
Naperville, Illinois, September 4, 2000*

THE POPEYE PLANK

"I am what I am, and if people aren't willing to accept
me on that basis then, hell, vote for somebody else."

—U.S. News & World Report, *October 25, 1993*

Rummyisms

PREDICTION

"I would not say that the future is necessarily less predictable than the past. I think the past was not predictable when it started."

—The Pentagon, April 4, 2003

CHANNELING CHENEY

"I've got to go back and check you when you all—not you personally, but you plural—when you all quote me somehow. I find you have been you quoting me imperfectly. That's a euphemism."

—Nice, France, February 9, 2005

THE ARMY YOU HAVE

"You go to war with the army you have, not the army you might want or wish to have at a later time."

—Speaking to U.S. soldiers in Kuwait, December 8, 2004

IRON LAW

"It's essentially a matter of physics. It isn't a matter of money."

—On delays in adding armor to Army vehicles in Iraq, December 8, 2004

61

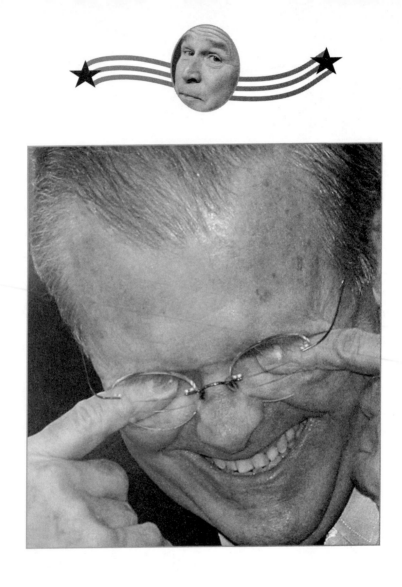

PRE-KNOWING

"I think what you'll find is whatever it is we do substantively, there will be near perfect clarity as to what it is. And it will be known, and it will be known to the Congress, and it will be known to you, probably before we decide it. But it will be known."

—The Pentagon, February 28, 2003

NOT KNOWING

"As we know, there are known knowns; there are things we know we know. We also know there are known unknowns; that is to say we know there are some things we do not know. But there are also unknown unknowns—the ones we don't know we don't know."

—The Pentagon, February 12, 2002

ON TRUTH

"If I know the answer, I'll tell you the answer,
and if I don't I'll just respond, cleverly."

—*Bagram Air Base, Afghanistan, April 27, 2002*

THE GROWING THREAT

"It's an enormous country. You know, it's bigger than Texas, or as big, I guess. I haven't looked lately."

—*On Iraq, The Pentagon, December 23, 2002*

DIGGER

"We do have a saying in America, if you're in a hole, stop digging. Um, I'm not sure I should have said that. Let's pretend I never said that."

—*The Pentagon, September 25, 2002*

HE SAID, HE SAID

"I believe what I said yesterday. I don't know what I said, but I know what I think and I assume it's what I said."

—*The Pentagon, February 21, 2002*

FREEDOM

"They know what they're doing, and they're doing a terrific job, and it's untidy, and freedom's untidy, and free people are free to make mistakes and commit crimes and do bad things. They're also free to live their lives and do wonderful things."

—The Pentagon, April 11, 2003

WHAT HAPPENS

"You're going to be told lots of things. You get told things every day that don't happen. It doesn't seem to bother people. It gets printed in the press. The world thinks all of these things happen. They never happen. Everyone is so eager to get the story before, in fact, the story is there, that the world is constantly being fed things that haven't happened. All I can tell you is, it hasn't happened."

—The Pentagon, February 28, 2003

BOX

"You know, it's the old glass box at the—at the gas station, where you're using those little things trying to pick up the prize, and you can't find it. It's—and it's all these arms are going down in there, and so you keep dropping it and picking it up again and moving it, but— some of you are probably too young to remember those— those glass boxes, but—but they used to have them at all the gas stations when I was a kid."

—The Pentagon, December 6, 2001

FLYING MACHINE

"The American people have been able to live in a free
society for a lot of decades, and amazingly they have a
good inner gyroscope. They get blown by the winds, to
be sure, and all the bad news, and they get disturbed
and concerned and down. And then it balances out,
they figure it out, and sometimes the carburetor
gets flooded, if you will, but it doesn't take long
for them to sort through all that stuff."

—Al Asad, Iraq, October 10, 2004

MILITARY INTELLIGENCE

"Oh my goodness gracious, what you can buy off the
Internet in terms of overhead photography. A trained
ape can know an awful lot of what is going on in
this world, just by punching on his mouse,
for a relatively modest cost."

—The Pentagon, June 12, 2001

JADED

"That characterization is so far from the mark that I am shocked—sort of."

—*The Pentagon, March 21, 2002*

BEING

"Once in a while, I'm standing here, doing something and I think, 'What in the world am I doing here?' It's a big surprise."

—*Interview with* The New York Times, *May 16, 2001*

NOTHINGNESS

"Things will not be necessarily continuous. The fact that they are something other than perfectly continuous ought not to be characterized as a pause. There will be some things that people will see. There will be some things that people won't see. And life goes on."

—*The Pentagon, October 12, 2001*

71

About the Author

JACOB WEISBERG is the editor of *Slate* magazine. He has been a commentator for *All Things Considered* and a contributing writer for *The New York Times Magazine* and *Vanity Fair*. He is also the author, with Robert E. Rubin, of *In an Uncertain World*.

PHOTO CREDITS

AP/Wide World Photos: vi, 40, 43

Corbis: xvii, 5, 9, 31, 45

Getty: ii (top row, left; third row, left and right, fourth row, center), xv, xxi (top), 2, 6, 13, 16, 19, 23, 32, 35, 39, 50, 53, 62

Landov: running head photo, ii (top row, center and right; second row, all; third row, center; fourth row, left and right), xi, xiv, xxi (bottom), xxii, 1, 10, 15, 20, 24, 27, 36, 46, 51, 54, 57, 58, 59, 61, 64, 67, 68, 71, 72